Quit Hogging the Road!

Olin T. Gideonson

Quit Hogging the Road!

Copyright 2007 by Olin T. Gideonson
All Rights Reserved

To order copies of this book, send check or money order payable to Outpost Delta for $15.95 plus $4.00 shipping and handling ($19.95 total) to:

Outpost Delta
P.O. Box 2254
Corvallis, OR 97339-2254

Inquiries regarding special discounts for bulk purchases and author engagements also may be sent to the above address or e-mailed to outpostdelta@peak.org.

ISBN 978-1-60530-302-4

Printed in the United States of America

February 2008

Dedication

To my wife, a very kind, wise, and supportive partner, who knows the relative importance of self, spouse, family, and home to work, peace, justice, community, and environment.

Acknowledgments

Trickster Vickster and Frog Woman for their expert production help.

Contents

Preface

1.	Form and Function	1
2.	Units of Measure	6
3.	Speed and Collisions	19
4.	Empty Space	28
5.	Untapped Power	35
6.	Sledgehammers and Nails	45
7.	Your Choice	57
8.	Motown Spirit	73
9.	Uncle Sam's Garage	83

Preface

Advances in electronics and telecommunications over the last 50 years have transformed our civilization's ability to transmit information. These advances are characterized by increased efficiency and miniaturization of components making up the information superhighway. In contrast, our civilization's transportation system for products and people has become less efficient and grown larger. We have more freeway lanes to carry more automobiles that are essentially the same size as the first horseless carriage of a century ago. We are overloading the atmosphere with carbon dioxide from our cars and trucks while building more roads to accommodate ever more of them. Times have changed. *Why hasn't our transportation system?*

The vision of this book is that in 15 years you will see most people driving much smaller cars to work everyday. You will see traffic flow in special high-volume corridors improved by various lane management techniques, known as intelligent transportation system (ITS) and active traffic management (ATM) technologies. More so than today, vehicles will be segregated in lanes according to type and destination, and taxed for usage according to purpose and engine type/size/fuel.

My premise is that we need more choices for our personal transportation and more efficient use of our travel lanes. One size doesn't fit all purposes. If you have a big family car, why not have a small personal one, too? To drive a big 4-6 passenger car without passengers is hogging the space available on the road. It is a luxury for which as a society we can no longer afford to build infrastructure. It is highly inefficient, and just plain stupid and wasteful, to build a transportation system to accommodate vehicles that are five-sixths empty. Driving a conventional-size car by oneself is being a true road hog.

This book is about the automobile and highway system as we know them today, have known them for decades, and could know them in the near future. This book is a vehicle itself. Its purpose is to take you to a place in your mind where you can see an alternative to just more of the same cars and traffic congestion in the future. You are encouraged to visit the several websites noted at the end of each chapter for additional information and visual content.

Many consumers are concerned about high gasoline costs, foreign oil dependency, and global warming. Hybrid-fueled cars are a step in the right direction, but commuting in a hybrid Cadillac Escalade won't get us to where we need to go to meet our energy independence and climate change goals. A smaller, more fuel-efficient car is only part of the solution. Is today's Smart Car smart enough? No. While mini cars are good for fuel efficiency, this book explains why battery-powered micro cars—with only two seats in tandem--are better for relieving traffic congestion and halting human-induced climate change.

Increasing the efficiency of the whole transportation system operation is the key. There simply aren't enough public funds or right-of-way to build all the travel lanes needed to serve the vehicles in our urban areas. Parking also can be more efficient and more widely available if every space in a city is not designed to accommodate the big cars and pick-up trucks.

Choice is good, and we need more options to reduce congestion and green house gas emissions. Today's automobile designs <u>are</u> changing to respond to energy issues, but time is running out to make the paradigm shift needed before we reach gridlock and irreversible climate change. We need a vehicle that has the creature comforts of a car but takes up the lane space of a bicycle, motorcycle, or scooter—and uses as little fossil fuel as possible.

Most American households now own two or more cars. For family trips, keep your SUV or whatever full-size vehicle you might have, but as soon as you can, buy something that is roughly as wide as you are for getting to work and doing shopping. As economist Ernest Schumacher famously said and wrote in 1973, "Small is beautiful." It still is. Time's up. Plan on downsizing one of your cars.

Supply follows demand. Demand change—from manufacturers and government. A sustainable, efficient transportation system will be good for your wallet, health, and planet.

–OTG

Quit Hogging the Road!

Olin T. Gideonson

1. Form and Function

Evolution of the Horseless Carriage

The automobile is an environmentally controlled, enclosed space, designed for safety, comfort, speed, and cargo (people or goods). We put ourselves inside a hard-shelled pod—some are even called "beetles"—to get from here to there. We warm or cool our pod for comfort. We like to be out of the weather some days with windows up or air conditioner on, and immersed in it other days with windows down and sunroof open. Besides the outside color of the shell, options inside are many, as are manufacturers and vehicle types, all contributing to a sense of *personalized transport.*

We drive for a purpose, but also for the fun and personal freedom of it.

We like to listen to our favorite music or to talk-radio while in transit. We may want to take a few things along with us or pick them up along the way. And more often than not, whether for work or shopping, we go it <u>alone </u>or perhaps with one other person.

However, the size and form of our pod was not purposefully designed for the function it has in 2007. It has evolved but is largely unchanged from a form-following-function started over 100 years ago. Are you still driving your great grandfather's hay wagon to the city? You might work in an office or store today, but it was farmers in 19th-century America who used their hay wagons for everything from transporting the family from farm to church on Sunday mornings to picking up sacks of flour and sugar at the mercantile in town.

The very first automobiles invented were basically engine-powered wagons and buggies—"horseless carriages."

Today, the farming rural life has been replaced by the commuting urban life for most people. Were it not for the invention of the automobile we'd probably be just riding a horse instead of hitching a horse to wagon to get to our jobs in town. It would be a lot less hassle and quicker.

Why are so many of us still driving the hay wagon everywhere when merely a buggy or horseback would suffice?

When people were fewer and lived in the country, there was lots of room for picking your path to town and pasturing or liverying your horse and wagon. There was lots of open country to pick a route. Where one person blazed a trail through forest or prairie, others followed a common path. With increasing people and traffic over time, rutted wagon tracks across the open range and along fence lines were graded, graveled, and paved to become two-lane or more "thoroughfares" carrying cars and trucks (driven still today by "teamsters"). Roads weren't designed to be 10-12 feet wide, they just evolved that way through wear on the landscape from wagon wheels.

If you were lucky enough to arrive safely with your cargo and without a broken wagon wheel, finding a place to securely park your wagon and rest your horse on the city streets was a problem. To meet the need, blacksmiths, who shoed horses anyway, opened and operated livery stables for a fee; these establishments later were transformed into parking lots, gas stations, and multi-story garages for our cars. What's really changed?

Today's automobile design, in terms of size and versatility, is still very similar to great grandfather's hay wagon, even though most people have left farm life and now commute to jobs in town. Traffic congestion and accidents in our metropolitan areas are an everyday occurrence. These daily commuting events are given routine news coverage every bit as important as the everyday news of yesteryear. Weather reports were an essential element of farming success and getting crops planted on time. Similarly, traffic reports today, provided by circling aircraft and remote cameras, are an essential element of commuting success and getting to work on time.

2. Units of Measure

Level of Service, Volume to Capacity Ratio, Speed, Weight and Wear

The ability of our highways to move vehicles from point A to point B is measured by traffic engineers in terms of three variables:

- Average travel speed
- Density
- Flow rate

These variables are used as measures of effectiveness to define the overall "level of service" (LOS). Los is a qualitative estimate of the performance efficiency of transportation facilities. LOS is evaluated according to a school-grade type of scoring where "A" is best, "C" is just OK, and "F" is failing.

Generally, a grade of "D" indicates traffic conditions that are significantly constraining free flow of movement (e.g., lane changes) and speed, and when traffic engineers consider adding lanes or other traffic management methods to increase the LOS. A grade of "E" can be described as crawling along, while "F" indicates stop-and-go or stalled movement.

Traffic congestion LOS standards have been developed and revised by the Transportation Research Board (TRB), as described in their *Highway Capacity Manual*. One of the TRB systems uses traffic volume on the road and the maximum capacity of that road to define a ratio, called the volume to capacity (v/c) ratio, which can be classified by degree of congestion. The *Highway Capacity Manual* (page 3-8) explains LOS:

> "Freeway operating characteristics include a wide range of rates of flow over which speed is relatively constant. This means that speed alone is not adequate as a performance measure by which to define level of service.
>
> Although speed is a major concern of drivers with respect to service quality, freedom to maneuver and proximity to vehicles are equally important parameters. These other qualities are directly related to the *density* of the freeway traffic stream. Further, rate of flow increases with increasing density throughout the full range of stable flows.
>
> For these reasons, density is the parameter used to define levels of service for basic

freeway segments. The densities used to define the various levels of service (LOS) are as follows:

LEVEL OF SERVICE	MAXIMUM DENSITY (PC/MI/LN)*
A	12
B	20
C	30
D	42
E	67
F	>67

* NUMBER OF PERSONAL CARS PER MILE PER LANE

These values are boundary conditions representing the maximum allowable densities for the associated level of service. The LOS-E boundary of 67 pc/mi/ln has been generally found to be the *critical density* at which capacity most often occurs. This corresponds to an average travel speed of 30 mph and a capacity of 2,000 pcphpl (passenger cars per hour per lane) for 60-mph and 70-mph design speeds. The exact speed and density, however, at which capacity occurs may vary somewhat from location to location."

Regardless of "official" measures, each motorist has their own LOS in mind, depending on how they feel that day and how important it is to get to their destination on time. It is no surprise that as more vehicles crowd into each travel lane, the speed of travel is significantly reduced while crash rates increase as drivers tailgate.

We all have seen that as traffic volumes increase, drivers tend to ignore maintaining a safe distance between cars--the rule of thumb of <u>at least</u> one car length per 10 mph of speed under <u>ideal</u> conditions. We drive like we're in big, carnival-type bumper cars, where it won't matter, nor would we mind, if we were to collide. And collide we do, often, during rush hour.

On the other hand, we like our distance from each other, enveloped in our steel and glass pods, feeling safe to stare at the car next to us, if not curse its driver, for cutting us off in our lane. When we get to work or back home after "battling" stop-and-go traffic, how do we feel about our highway's level of service?

Carpooling can increase our perception of level of service for drivers as well as passengers. As a passenger, one can read a book, listen to music, engage in conversation, and enjoy the scenery rather that battle traffic. As a driver, carpooling in most metropolitan areas can increase actual LOS as well as driver satisfaction by the use of high-occupancy vehicle (HOV) lanes—"diamond lanes."

HOV lanes are restricted to at least two persons per vehicle or, in some states, motorcycles. However, after more than 20 years of carpooling advocacy and lane construction, we see that most HOV lanes are underutilized in terms of vehicle potential occupancy or number of vehicles (which is good for those using them). On the other hand, we seem to have an unlimited ability to quickly fill to capacity new, unrestricted travel lanes with driver-only vehicles. If a measure of transportation performance were vehicles served per dollar invested, HOV lanes unfortunately seem to be the least cost-effective, except perhaps during peak periods.

Studies show that for an added HOV lane to be successful there must be a sufficient number of HOVs already traveling on the route. For the addition of an HOV third lane in either direction to a road with two existing mixed-flow lanes, the fraction of existing HOVs must be on the order of 30 percent of the vehicles (J. W. Dahlgren, *The Prospects for High Occupancy Toll (HOT) Lanes: Where Should They Be Implemented?* Final Report for MOU 361, Institute of Transportation Studies, Berkeley, 2001).

Consumer choice still favors the personal freedom of driving alone.

Another unit of measure not often considered by the everyday commuter is the weight of vehicles using our highways. Everyone driving a vehicle contributes to the wearing down of pavement and the cost of maintaining it. The heavier the vehicle, the more tires, the more wear. Today there are heavier trucks and cars on the road than ever before, and more of them. Sedans, pickup trucks, and sport utility vehicles (SUVs) vary in weight from approximately 1 to almost 4 tons. Tractor-trailers ("semis") hauling freight on our highways used to top-out at around 86,000 pounds, while today their weight often approaches 105,000 pounds. Many bridges were not designed 50 years ago for today's truck weights, and compounded by high speeds, cracks in girders are becoming commonplace.

Add to that wear the incredible grinding of pavement by studded snow tires, and we end up with ruts in travel lanes, creating dual rivers of water that hydroplane our cars. The allowance of snow tires on cars during winter months in climates that perhaps get one week of severe snow or ice per year is extremely costly to our roadways. It is another example of how we senselessly indulge ourselves in bigness and lazy convenience without realizing the cost that all of us pay.

The level of service declines while we hold onto a high level of indulgence.

Our roads are wearing out. There's not enough money to fix them. Perhaps that's why so many people have been buying SUVs and trucks with big tires that are designed for the "off-road" ruts, potholes, and rocks, which are increasingly encountered in the streets and highways of today.

Today's proposed solutions to funding highway improvements by allocating costs to users raise some fundamental issues about "free" use of the system. With congestion pricing, the idea is if you can increase the cost to users, demand and thus congestion will go down. In a democracy, is it right that only those who are more able to afford to travel on a highway are allowed to? Also, is it right to enable the more affluent to choose more polluting ways of travel, while the less affluent are expected to take mass transit? Should those who drive a large car with only the driver pay the same as carpoolers or other more efficient users? If the goal with ramp metering and tolling is to maintain mobility by restricting the number of vehicles to a certain capacity level, than perhaps it would be more equitable on a first-come, first-on basis. When a new facility needs to be financed, should the cost be spread amongst all potential users through a gas tax or car registration fees, or the cost targeted to only the specific users through a toll? What do people prefer, a tax or a toll? Neither is not an option that can fund maintenance of our existing highway system nor make improvements leading to greater efficiency.

Gas taxes have not been allowed to increase with the rate of inflation. Such increases are often voted down in referendums. The result is we can no longer afford to maintain the highways we have built over the last 50 years, let alone add more lanes to relieve congestion—if that would ever happen. In many cases, the construction of additional capacity induces more traffic and quickly absorbs it.

Studies have shown that when road capacity is increased, total travel time ultimately equalizes over time at the previous levels of congestion due to a triple convergence of dimensional shifts, due to drivers who previously:

- Used alternative routes during peak hours switch to the improved roadway (*spatial convergence*)

- Traveled just before or after the peak hour start to travel during those hours (*time convergence)*
- Used public transportation during peak hours now switch to driving, since it has become faster (*modal convergence*).

A study by University of London Centre for Transport Studies researcher Robert B. Noland, "Relationships Between Highway Capacity and Induced Vehicle Travel" (Transportation Research Part A 35 (2001) 47±72, July 1999) regarding the relationship between vehicle miles traveled (VMT) and additional capacity concludes that:

> "The results of the analyses presented clearly demonstrate that the hypothesis of induced demand cannot be rejected. Increased capacity clearly increases vehicle miles of travel beyond any short run congestion relief that may be obtained. The methods employed all found statistically significant relationships between lane miles and VMT. While other factors, such as

population growth, also drive increases in VMT, capacity additions account for about one quarter of this growth. This contribution to VMT growth has significant impacts on various environmental goals. For example, increasing U.S. highway capacity at historical rates may result in up to 43 million metric tons of carbon emissions compared to a complete freeze on adding additional lane miles. Constructing new lane miles at half the current rate might reduce carbon emissions proportionally."

Building more travel lanes leads to more vehicle miles traveled and net increases in carbon dioxide emissions. A report by Sightline Institute (Increases in Greenhouse Gas Emissions from Highway Widening Projects, Clark Williams-Derry, October 2007) concludes:

"Our estimates suggest that, over the course of five decades, adding new highway lanes will lead to substantial increases in vehicle travel and CO2 emissions from cars and trucks. Claims about fuel savings from congestion relief may hold slim merit over horizons of a decade or less. But over the long term, new traffic will fill the added road space, leading to long-term increases in vehicle emissions totaling tens of thousands of tons per lane-mile."

Thus, expansion of roadway capacity often does not decrease for long the rush-hour periods of frustrating slow speeds. The Surface Transportation Policy Project shows that providing a choice of transportation modes, such as bus and light rail transit, is the key to reducing congestion. Ironically, it is congestion that also encourages the use of other transportation modes.

For additional information, see:

www.sightline.org

www.transact.org/reports/tti2001/default.htm

3. Empty Space

More Room Than We Realize

As discussed in the previous chapter, density is an important factor in determining the level of service (LOS) of our highways. Therefore, it makes sense to examine if the space occupied by vehicles in each lane is being used efficiently.

Here's a simple test. The next time you drive somewhere, *count how many cars in the opposite lane have more than two persons inside.*

Why do we transport empty space and take it up on the road?

A standard, paved lane of roadway is 12 feet wide, and they usually come in pairs, one lane or more in each direction of travel. On either side of the travel lane(s), the standard is a 10-foot paved shoulder, although conformance with that standard varies considerably depending on the age and function of the roadway.

Our earliest roads often had no paved shoulder or shoulder at all, while today's roads may have shoulders designed for bicycles, breakdowns, and emergency vehicles. We use paint on the pavement or a physical barrier to separate lanes of travel, and signs as needed to indicate the proper direction. We encourage trucks and slower traffic to keep to the right lane on multi-laned roadways to allow the faster and smaller vehicles to pass on the left. However, with the volume of trucks on highways today, truck passing truck or even truck passing car is a common use of the center lane, contributing to uneven flow.

A typical passenger vehicle is about 6 feet wide, allowing a clear space in each lane of 3 feet on both sides of the vehicle (Figure 1), or 6 feet of clear space between vehicles with a paint stripe down the middle.

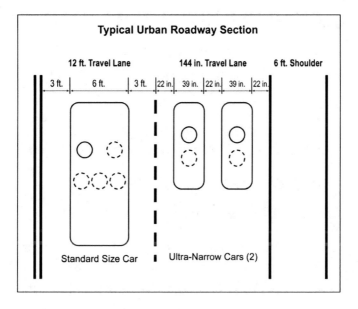

Figure 1.Typical Urban Roadway Section

We hurtle down the road, passing vehicles whose drivers sit a comfortable 12 feet away from us, person to person. Beside the driver in the front compartment, separated usually by the gear shift and parking brake in today's cars, sits the front passenger, if there is one.

In the rear compartment, there may be room for two or three additional passengers. If the vehicle carries only the driver, the space in the rear of the vehicle is underutilized as is the space in the lane width. However, it is the front passenger seat that is the highest value area in terms of wasted space when it is not occupied.

Placing a passenger first behind the driver instead of next to the driver (in tandem formation) would be the highest order of travel-lane space efficiency.

Sedans and SUVs vary in length from 13 to 20 feet. Pickup trucks can be 15 to 22 feet long. All of these are approximately 6 feet wide. The space occupied by these vehicles ranges from 78 square feet to 132 square feet. Thus, one person, the driver, can take up almost twice as much room on the highway as someone else. That is, the efficient utilization of space of the smaller car is twice that of the larger car. Put a passenger into the smaller vehicle, and the space efficiency becomes four times. The point of this exercise is to show that the driver that occupies more space, and the car that puts more wear on the road due to its weight, does so to the detriment of everyone else and incurs no significant additional expense other than through, typically, lost fuel efficiency. We allow that to be the case, except where we have built HOV lanes.

Some people question the safety of two ultra-narrow vehicles (UNVs) passing each other in a 6-foot half-lane with a distance between them of about 2 feet (Figure 1). However, consider that 2 feet is about the same distance between two 8.5-foot wide tractor-trailers with mirrors protruding 9 inches on each side and traveling in adjacent 12-foot lanes. (Some urban highways with only 11-foot lanes accommodate trucks.) Moreover, when two 50-foot long tractor-trailers occupy adjacent lanes at 67 mph, the time they are side-by-side with potential to collide ranges between 67 to 100 percent of the time of a 1- to 2-second breaking delay; whereas, two 8-foot long UNVs are only side-by-side from 8 to 16 percent of the breaking delay time. When one whole lane is used for only a single person in a car, 1,400-2,600 square feet of freeway space is needed for a car traveling at 67 mph with a breaking delay of 1-2 seconds. Even if lanes were too narrow for UNV's to travel side-by-side, travel in a staggered left-right formation in one lane with careful passing would be possible.

Through everyday observation, we know that most personal cars on our highways and city streets (as high as 85 to 90 percent of them) are carrying only the driver. One car for one person in one lane. Does that make sense? Why aren't there more vehicle options available besides a bike, motorcycle, or scooter?

Let's not forget that we normally don't drive indefinitely—eventually, when we reach our destination, we must park. If you want to park your vehicle on the street, the standard parallel parking space is 19 feet long by 9 feet wide, curb to travel lane. Parked, at zero speed, we can put our cars side by side with just enough room to open the doors so that drivers and passengers can exit their vehicles. Parallel parking is the least desirable of all types because of the danger of opening doors next to the travel lane and the maneuverability skills needed. Angle parking of 30- or 45-degrees is slightly more efficient and safe because it takes less room to maneuver into the space, and doors open between parking spaces not into the travel lane.

Before leaving the topic of empty space and density, the problem of urban sprawl's contribution to traffic congestion is worthy of discussion. Since the end of World War II, the pattern of U.S. development has been on the assumption that people will use cars to get to everywhere they want to go, and new, low-density housing belongs on the cheapest land, often farmland, that is farthest from urban centers and services.

Only one-quarter of the increase in vehicle miles traveled over the last 25 years is attributable to population growth.

Land is being consumed at a rate three times faster than population growth. That means longer trips (through undeveloped empty space) and people driving alone (with unoccupied empty space) are by far the greatest contributors to demands on our transportation system. (See "Measuring Sprawl and Its Transportation Impacts," *Journal of the Transportation Research Board*, Vol. 1832, 2003, and FHWA *Highway Statistics 2005.*)

In conclusion, density is one but a very important measure of the safety, capacity, and efficiency of our highways. The primary variable of travel lane efficiency as well as parking efficiency **is *the size of the vehicle itself.*** And if our future land development patterns were more compact and less sprawling, achieved by following the principles of Smart Growth, there would be fewer big cars on our urban highways taking up unnecessary space.

Visit:

www.smartgrowthamerica.org

www.aaafoundation.org

www.sensibletransportation.org

www.transact.org

4. Speed and Collisions

Fast and Big, Ever Popular

Passenger automobiles are designed to cruise at 70 mph on our highways. An object such as a car that weighs approximately 4,000 pounds and travels at 70 mph is governed by certain laws of physics (as is everything) if it is to remain stable and controllable by a driver. Throughout the history of the automobile, we have seen cars designed having four wheels, three wheels (two in front or back), front-wheel drive and rear-wheel drive, nine passenger to two passenger, high center of gravity and low center of gravity, streamlined and blunt-nosed.

Each of these designs has trade-offs in terms of its ability to deal with the physics of motion and perform the specific purpose for which it was designed. By necessity, the design of a nine-passenger shuttle van is going to be different, at least in size, than a two-passenger sports car. Regardless, each vehicle must negotiate turns at highway speeds and for collision avoidance; thus, their design must address the forces attributable to mass and velocity.

Vehicle manufacturers have not always recognized or appropriately balanced the trade-offs of vehicle function and stability—nor fuel efficiency. The problem of roll-over demonstrated by the earliest SUVs (army jeeps) as well as more recent models has been well documented. Electronic stability control (ESC) is now mandated by federal safety standards for many vehicle models to limit the possibility of roll-over.

A vehicle's center of gravity is the key determinant of its vulnerability to roll-over.

The higher the center of gravity, the wider the vehicle's wheel base (width) must be to mitigate for roll-over. For example, a "wide-track" is seen as desirable for sports cars to improve handling on curves. However, another way to compensate for high-speed turns is to keep the center of gravity very low, regardless of an exceptionally wide wheel base. Even the narrowest of vehicles resist tipping over if most of the weight is near the ground.

Most full-size cars weigh approximately 4,000 pounds (2 tons) and typically transport in a commuting scenario only one 200-pound person. That's a vehicle weight to payload ratio of 200 to 1. Would anyone argue that is efficient? Why do we find that ratio acceptable when the cost of fuel to move that mass is increasingly expensive? One reason is we seek safety in bulk. Survival of the biggest. We've all seen the results of collisions between small cars and bigger cars. We must share the road with big trucks. Do drivers of Humvees envision themselves on a freeway battlefield?

The severity of collisions is a simple matter of physics, involving velocity, mass, momentum, inertia, and energy absorption. The greater the mass of an object times its velocity, the greater the force applied to another object upon impact. The force (kinetic energy) that might move the object upon impact must overcome the inertia of the object if it is fixed, or momentum if it is in motion, both of which are a function of its mass. Some of that force can be absorbed by either object as they might be crushed upon impact. When billiard balls strike each other, the momentum of one is transferred to the other, less that lost due to friction on the table and air resistance.

Consider what happens when a 10-ton truck hits a 2-ton car at rest versus a 1-ton car at rest. The added inertia from the mass of the larger car being struck might result in a greater force being applied as compared to a smaller car that might more easily move from the impact. There are many structural factors involved that contribute to driver/passenger safety in such situations.

All car models sold in the U.S. today must undergo crash tests to evaluate their safety, unless they are not fully assembled and sold as kits. Manufacturers have been required by federal government safety standards to provide safety restraints (lap and shoulder belts) and driver and front passenger air bags, among other measures. Options include side curtain air bags. Reinforced side panels and columns inside and between doors provide additional side impact protection. Front and rear panels are designed to be energy absorbing, including crumple zones, to lessen the shock of impact. And bumpers, well, some are better than others at even low speed impacts, and have not consistently met standards.

In spite of all these safety features, it is surprising for most people that passenger vehicles with their air bags *et al.* are not as safe in a crash as many race cars with their roll cages, crossing seat belt systems, and helmeted drivers. Even small vehicles equipped with such race car features can provide a driver with the safety of a much larger vehicle.

The Smart Car, a European import, employs a safety management system called the tridion safety cell. The cell protects occupants with three layers of steel that are reinforced at strategic points. Both doors are also reinforced with steel bars. The car's design, reinforced doors, and wheel bases allow for impact absorption and redistribution of crash energy.

Safety is largely a matter of perception. Who would dare to feel safe in a situation where cars approach each other in opposite directions at 60 mph separated only by six feet and a paint stripe? But we do it everyday.

Regardless of the size of the vehicle, safety ultimately relies on driver awareness and defensive techniques. The American Trucking Association has been proactive in trying to educate car drivers about sharing the road with big trucks. Their program emphasizes being aware of trucks' blind spots, keeping a safe following distance, and passing with a safe distance.

Visit:

www.nhtsa.dot.gov

5. Untapped Power

Energy Is Everywhere

To move a lot of mass takes a lot of power. Horsepower is a term commonly associated with the size and equivalent power of internal combustion engines, for example, V-8, 3.5 liter, and hemi car engines. Horsepower also is used to measure the power generated by electric motors. Electricity powered vehicles have many more advantages than gasoline, diesel, natural gas, or hydrogen powered vehicles.

In fact, the one and only drawback to electric power in the past has been the limited range due to battery discharge as the power is consumed. Charging batteries every 20-40 miles, which can take from 2-8 hours with a 120-volt supply, is an inconvenience for long-distance trips. With a 200-amp 220-volt power supply, lead-acid batteries can be charged to 80 percent in only 10 minutes. However, the use today of more exotic metals in batteries, load controllers, and electronic chargers has improved on past battery technologies, and future improvements are expected.

Lithium ion batteries can now provide electric cars with a range of over 100 miles and quick recharge.

For example, recently developed at Stanford's Department of Materials Science and Engineering is a method based on nanotechnology that has potential to increase the life of rechargeable lithium ion batteries to almost two days. A team led by Assistant Professor Yi Cui developed a substitute material for the graphite used for the anode in today's laptop computer batteries. Their new material uses silicon nanowires arranged in a sponge-like network that is grown directly on a metallic substrate that collects current.

Large lithium ion and metal halide batteries are becoming less expensive and can greatly improve the range and charging time of electric vehicles. Nevertheless, lead-acid batteries are a proven technology with plenty of low-cost availability. For neighborhood, within town trips—even daily commutes of less than 40 miles--lead-acid batteries are perfectly suitable. Charging stations for electric vehicles could be made widely available at places of employment and parking garages. California already has hundreds of charging stations at Costco stores, Kaiser hospitals, and BART transit stations. Tire stores could have 200-amp 220-volt charging stations, or quickly replace drained battery packs with charge ones like they change tires.

Electric charging station.

Electric motors need no energy-draining torque converters or gear-shifting to transfer power to a car's wheels. This gives tremendous acceleration to a car compared to one with an internal combustion engine. As a measure of performance, time in seconds from 0 to 60 mph is a standard of the automobile industry. In spite of such superior performance, the electric car, except for hybrid versions pairing an electric motor with a small internal combustion engine, has not been embraced by the automobile industry. **Detroit's approach has been to take a standard-sized, heavy car and power it with heavy lead-acid batteries.** For an interesting history of electric cars, read the book "Who Killed the Electric Car" or see www.whokilledtheelectriccar.com or the movie (now on DVD).

The drawbacks of hydrocarbon-based fuels are becoming more relevant as oil supplies peak, fuel prices increase, and carbon-dioxide accumulates in our atmosphere. Every gallon of gasoline burned contributes 20 pounds of carbon dioxide to the atmosphere.

The technical strides achieved over the last 40 years in limiting smog and other air pollutants from internal combustion engines are being eclipsed by the ever-increasing number of vehicles on the road. This is true not only in the United States, but even more so in developing countries and booming economic giants such as China and increasingly India.

Even a 20 percent reduction in greenhouse gas emissions (GHG) in 2007, as is called for in the Kyoto Protocol, only takes us back to the same, unacceptable levels of 1990. Yet, carbon dioxide (a leading GHG) is projected to increase 41 percent from cars and light trucks (SUVs) over the next 20 years. Vehicle miles traveled in the United States is projected to increase 59 percent between 2005 and 2030, which far exceeds a projected population increase of 23 percent and a projected fuel economy increase of the nation's fleet of vehicles by only 12 percent (U.S. Department of Energy, Energy Information Administration, *Annual Energy Outlook 2007).*

Even with success at requiring an increase in fuel efficiency standards from 25 mpg to 35 mpg in 2020, carbon dioxide emissions by 2030 would still be 12 percent higher than in 2005 and 40 percent higher than in 1990. To achieve climate stabilization goals of a 60-80 percent in carbon dioxide emissions by 2050, we would need by 2020 at least 15 percent (perhaps up to 30 percent) lower levels than in 1990 (U.S. Department of Energy, Energy Information Administration, *Annual Energy Outlook 2007).* Therefore, it seems obvious that the only way we will stop global warming is to convert to vehicles that have exceptionally high equivalency of gasoline miles per gallon, on the magnitude of 100 miles per gallon, or quit driving so much.

We need to be driving cars getting the equivalent of 100 miles per gallon by 2020—or adopt other ways of getting around—to beat climate change.

It is worth noting that if U.S.-made cars had the same fuel efficiency as European-made cars, the U.S. would save the amount of oil it imports from the Middle East.

The benefits of turning away from a heavy reliance on fossil fuels have become a concern with electric power plants, also. Even in the northwest United States, rich with low-cost hydropower, approximately 60 percent of the region's electrical power originates from coal-fired and natural gas-fired power plants. While hydropower, solar cells, wind turbines, and geothermal wells tap unused renewable energy sources, the prospect of complete abandonment of using oil and coal for electrical generation is remote in the foreseeable future. This is true in spite of their contribution, along with our automobiles, to global warming from greenhouse gas emissions.

Electric vehicles can reduce total pollutant emissions by at least 50 percent (including carbon dioxide), even when considering power generation by coal. With power generation from natural gas, pollutants per mile are reduced 74 percent. With solar and wind generation, electric vehicles are virtually pollution free.

Much research of late has been devoted to finding alternatives to fossil fuels and conserving electrical energy. For gasoline engines, ethanol production from corn has only limited supply capability and increases food prices; other crops need to be added. Biodiesel has similar problems and potentials. A drawback of solar and wind power is the irregularity of the weather. The flow of water over dams is much more controllable with spillways, although total stored water is also dependent on weather. Hydropower managers are able to increase spillway flows and thus electric power to the grid whenever demand increases. Demand peaks during meal times and during extreme temperatures that prompt people to use electric heating and cooling. The design capacity of the power grid is predicated upon meeting peak demand. Thus, during many hours of the day, and especially at night when people are asleep, large amounts of power that are generated by dam spillways go untapped. The same would be true for strong winds turning turbine blades at night.

Charging electric vehicles at night while we sleep can tap large amounts of unused hydropower and wind power.

This is a perfect time to be cost effectively and efficiently charging electric vehicles for the next day's trip, which for 90 percent of commuters in urban areas going to and from work, is a distance under 20 miles.

For more information on electric cars, hybrid cars, climate change, and energy efficiency, visit:

www.electrifyingtimes.com
www.Fev-now.com

www.eaaev.org

www.rmi.org

www.ase.org

www.greenercars.org

www.pewclimate.org

www.greencarcongress.org

www.sightline.org

www.drivelesslivemore.org

www.eia.doe.gov/oiaf/aeo/index.html

6. Sledgehammers and Nails

Picking the Right Tool for the Job

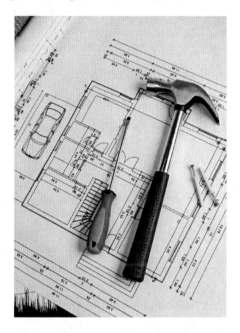

Would a carpenter build a house using only a sledgehammer, instead of a framing hammer, to pound the nails?

Would a skydiver wear a hoop-skirt instead of a jumpsuit?

Would a businessman wear a size 48-long suitcoat if he were only 5-foot-6-inches?

Ridiculous to think about, isn't it? Then why would a commuter drive a Hummer instead of a Beetle? Some things just don't make sense to do. It typifies extravagance, waste, and thoughtlessness in our culture, and not something the world should emulate. Big is not always better, by any means. And small can be beautiful. *It depends on the purpose.*

It just makes sense to pick the right tool to do the job. And if the right tool doesn't exist, invent it. That's the American way.

The marketplace of cars and our choices have been influenced by being drunk on cheap gasoline for decades. It has become normal life for each of us to needlessly, wastefully emit tons of carbon dioxide and pollutants to the atmosphere. The costs of our binge are becoming evident.

What's so "modern" about today's automobile when compared to the astounding innovations and efficiencies developed in the consumer electronics industry? We have gone from tubes to transistors to chips to nanotechnics. Miniaturization and microtechnology have been a common theme for popular electronic goods.

Energy efficiency built into our latest home appliances has made it possible to serve our growing population without adding gigawatts of energy generation facilities. These improved, redesigned appliances (marketed with energy efficiency ratings) and the adoption of electricity conservation measures have prevented the widespread brown-outs predicted for the 1990s by the electric utility companies and nuclear power plant proponents.

- Remember the size of the first cellular phones?
- Remember the memory capacity and size of the first personal computers?
- Remember the first microwave ovens?
- Remember the first portable music players (the Walkman)?

- Remember the size of the first digital projectors?
- Remember the capabilities of the first electronic calculators?

Evidently, we have become very good at doing more with less in the United States of America—except for the automobile.

Consider modern telephony and the internet. There are many similarities between modern telephony and our highway system. Both are highly linear and move things in streams of bits. DSL in telephony stands for "Digital Subscriber Line." DSL telephony doesn't necessarily require new wiring; it can use the phone line you already have. With HOV lanes, we have essentially added another wire to the phone system for internet use only. This is expensive and inefficient and not supported widely by the users. How can it be made more efficient? Perhaps we need DSL for highways – "Divided Single Lanes"—where two small vehicles can run together side-by-side by halving the standard 12-foot lane.

An ultranarrow vehicle, the Tango (Photo: Commuter Cars Corporation)

A DSL connection is able to move more information through a standard phone line while also allowing you to make regular telephone calls, even when you're online. The copper wires have lots of room for carrying more than your phone conversations -- they are capable of handling a much greater bandwidth, or range of frequencies, than that demanded for voice.

DSL for the internet exploits this "extra capacity" to carry information on the wire without disturbing the line's ability to carry conversations. Modern equipment that sends digital rather than analog data can safely use much more of the telephone line's capacity. The entire plan is based on matching particular frequencies to specific tasks.

Just as our computers send information in packets of bits or "bytes" via the internet, our traffic lanes carry cars and trucks filled with goods and people via the interstate highway system. Except our traffic management system is rather chaotic. The problem is we are not using the "bandwidth" of our highways efficiently—our cars are packets that don't carry enough bits (passengers). If we won't pack in more bits by ridesharing (and 30 years of efforts show most of us won't), than we should shrink the packets.

The internet also allocates certain frequencies to different types of traffic: voice and data, analog and digital. On our highways we are mixing all kinds of cars, recreational vehicles, and trucks together in the same lanes.

The frequencies of our highway system are jumbled.

Speeds are uneven; vehicles jockey for position. Pulses of slow-down/speed-up cars surge through the congested traffic lanes during rush hour. The Texas Transportation Institute estimates 5.7 billion gallons of fuel are wasted each year due to congestion (*2002 Urban Mobility Report*).

To improve the evenness of traffic flow, we could better enforce speeds, discourage aggressive driving, and encourage convoys of trucks having similar payloads to form at weigh stations and ports of entry. We could provide more slow-vehicle pull-outs and passing lanes going up hills. The number of trucks on the road is unsettling to many car drivers, as trucks jockey for position to maintain their speed under congested conditions.

We could allocate some traffic lanes exclusively to trucks, and other lanes to other types of vehicles. Some states are now considering restrictions on truck traffic on interstate freeways. For example, Florida has banned semi-trailer rigs from the fast lane (left lane) on stretches of three interstates. At least six other states in the mid-west and west are now considering construction of truck-only lanes, perhaps paid for by tolling, and segregation of trucks/cars.

The impetus for these actions has been the large increase in truck freight traffic in recent years resulting from increased imports and intermodal shipping through our ports. The expansion and maintenance of our nation's railway system to serve freight and passengers also has not kept pace and has added to highway congestion. For more information, visit www.freightrailworks.org.

Transportation departments at the state and federal levels are studying and implementing through trials various lane management strategies to more effectively and efficiently manage the flow of traffic on existing multi-lane highways.

Lane management strategies are ways to regulate travel demand, separate traffic streams to reduce turbulence, and utilize available and unused capacity.

The U.S. Department of Transportation, Federal Highway Administration (FHWA) has funded research in this area and published an overview titled, "Managed Lanes: A Primer" (FHWA-HOP-05-031). This FHWA publication is based on research at the Texas Transportation Institute by Tina Collier and Ginger Goodin (Managed Lanes: A Cross-Cutting Study, FHWA-HOP-05-037, November, 2004). Examples of operating managed lane projects include high-occupancy vehicle (HOV) lanes, value priced lanes, high occupancy toll (HOT) lanes, or exclusive or special use lanes. FHWA says that these early managed lane projects have proven successful, though relatively simple in design and operating conditions, and, by and large, have received widespread public support.

Managed lane strategies typically address pricing (tolls), vehicle eligibility, and access control.

Pricing includes both traditional toll lanes and toll lanes that use congestion pricing, where price is varied during certain time periods in order to manage demand (e.g., peak-period surcharge or off-peak discount). With *vehicle eligibility,* lanes are managed by allowing certain vehicles or restricting others. Besides HOV lanes, applications of vehicle eligibility may include exclusive truck lanes, bus lanes, ultra-narrow vehicle lanes, or truck-restricted lanes. A managed lane freeway could vary vehicle group eligibility over the course of a day serving, for example, commuter trips during peak periods and trucks at other times. An example of *access control* would be express lanes where all vehicles are allowed but access is limited during long stretches of the facility, minimizing turbulence in the flow of vehicles. More complicated managed lane facilities blend more than one of these strategies.

Managed lane strategies are applied to a "freeway-within-a-freeway." That is, a designated number of lanes within the freeway cross section are separated from the general-purpose lanes. Traffic operations and demand on the freeway are managed using a combination of tools and techniques to respond to changing conditions and continuously achieve an optimal condition, such as free-flow speeds.

An often incorporated tool for lane control is with overhead variable message signs (VMS), which indicate specific conditions and requirements for travel in individual lanes. Examples of how demand can be managed to meet performance objectives include:

- Raising the toll rate on a priced facility to maintain a speed of 60 mph

- Raising the occupancy requirement to use an HOV lane so that bus operating speeds of 50 mph can be maintained

- Closing an on-ramp to express lanes during peak periods so that the express lanes can operate within a volume threshold of 1500 vehicles per hour per lane.

European countries are ahead of the United States in implementing managed lane strategies. The FHWA report, "Active Traffic Management: The Next Step in Congestion Management," (FHWA-PL-07-012,

July, 2007) provides results of an investigation of strategies including speed harmonization, temporary shoulder use, and dynamic signing and rerouting, implemented by transportation agencies in Denmark, England, Germany, and the Netherlands. The research team, which was comprised largely of federal and state DOT officials (Mirshahi et al., as associated with American Trade Initiatives), has recommended that the U.S. should implement active traffic management and promote it by:

- Optimizing existing infrastructure during recurrent and non-recurrent congestion

- Emphasizing customer orientation

- Focusing on trip reliability

- Providing consistent messages to roadway users

- Making operations a priority in planning, programming, and funding processes.

7. Your Choice

One Medium and One Small, Please. No Supersize.

Yes, we have built compacts and "smart cars" of small size and high miles per gallon (available only in Europe until 2008—*why?*). And with rising gasoline prices and an environmental ethic, many people are choosing hybrid gasoline-electric cars. The manufacturers' inability to keep up with the demand for hybrids demonstrates a willingness of consumers to adopt new car technologies if they can see a benefit, such as reduced cost.

Unfortunately, the vast majority of consumers during the last 30 years have continued to choose to purchase the large SUV, minivan, luxury sedan, and pick-up truck with the big engine. For awhile during the gas crisis and OPEC embargo of the 1970's, as gas prices rose as now, consumer buying patterns turned toward more fuel-efficient cars. However, advances in fuel efficiency by U.S. manufacturers, and improvements to our national average, have been relatively minor compared to other countries.

- Do we need 6 or 8 cylinders, or would 3 or 4 get us to work just as well? The answer is obvious.

- Do we need passenger space for 4 or 5 when we drive to work alone or with one other person? The answer is obvious.

- Do we need the ability to drive 300 miles without refueling to go 20 miles roundtrip to and from work each day? The answer is obvious.

- Is it possible to indefinitely have increasing numbers of personal cars on the existing highway without sacrificing freight movement and safety? The answer is obvious.

For many years, traffic engineers and planners have implemented the idea of "high occupancy vehicle" (HOV) lanes—the diamond lanes on our freeways. While these have exclusively allocated a lane to passenger cars with two-or-more occupants, HOV lanes are rarely used to their design capacity. To convert an unrestricted lane to an HOV lane is to take away the capacity of a lane open to all vehicles. The simple fact is that HOV lanes, after decades of trial, have not changed the behavior of most commuters to adopt carpooling rather than driving by oneself. Most cars in HOV lanes are occupied by members of the same household unit. HOV lanes have not been effective (enough) in relieving traffic congestion nor encouraging widespread adoption of carpooling. The implementation of managed lane strategies could increase their efficiency.

We are losing the battle in the U.S. to convince more commuters to adopt alternative transportation, including transit, walking, biking, carpooling.

Long-term modal usage trends in the U.S. from 1980 to 2000 showed an increased portion of approximately 11 percent more workers driving alone to work.

That is, 64.37 percent of workers drove alone to work in 1980, and 75.70 percent of workers drove alone to work in 2000. Carpooling actually dropped more than 7 percent over 20 years from 19.73 percent to 12.19 percent. In fact, all forms of alternative transportation are used by a lower percentage than 20 years ago.

The only positive change nationwide is that more people are working at home; 2.25 percent in 1980 and 3.26 percent in 2000. (*Commuting in America*, NCHRP Report 550, Transportation Research Board, 2006, p. xvi). However, some states did do significantly better or worse than others. There were steep declines in carpooling rates in the mid-Atlantic states centered around Virginia; transit and carpooling increased sharply in the West. All states had between 73 and 83 percent solo drivers in 2000, except less in Alaska (67 percent), Hawaii 64 percent), and New York (56 percent).

To say that programs encouraging carpooling, biking, busing, and walking to work haven't worked or made a difference would be too severe. For example, worksites that participate in the Commute Trip Reduction program in Washington State remove more than 19,000 vehicles off of the roads each day, 13,480 trips in the Puget Sound region alone. Since the Commute Trip Reduction law took effect in 1993, the drive-alone rate has declined by nearly 10 percent at worksites in the program, from 69.7 percent in 1993 to 62.8 percent in 2003.

The last 40 years has shown an increase in the number of vehicles owned per household; although, the last 10 years has shown some stability. In 2000, 55 percent of U.S. households owned at least two cars compared to 21 percent in 1960. The percentage of households with three cars has remained steady at 17-18 percent since 1980, but more than tripled during the decade before that.

PERCENTAGE OF HOUSEHOLDS OWNING VEHICLES IN THE
UNITED STATES, 1960-2000

# VEHICLES	1960 (%)	1970 (%)	1980 (%)	1990 (%)	2000 (%)
0	21	18	12	11	10
1	58	48	36	34	35
2	19	29	34	37	38
3	2	5	18	18	17

SOURCE: *COMMUTING IN AMERICA*, NCHRP REPORT 550,
TRANSPORTATION RESEARCH BOARD, 2006, P. 39 (FIGURE 2-36)

About half of all American households now own two cars or more—more than double that in 1960.

Rising congestion is now a factor during our commutes in the smaller metro areas as well as the largest areas, especially during peak periods of travel (the rush hour commute). A study by the Texas Transportation Institute indicates that average delay per peak period traveler rose from 16 hours per year in 1982 to 46 hours per year in 2002. Congestion affected 33 percent of peak period travel in 1982 and 67 percent in 2002. Duration of time each day deemed congested on our highways was 4.5 hours in 1982 and 7 hours in 2002 (2004

Annual Urban Mobility Study, David Shank and Tim Lomax, Texas A&M University; *ibid,* p. 125.)

Congestion statistics indicate a worse condition in all three measures: intensity, extent, and duration.

We are traveling farther to get to work than we did 40 years ago, too. In 1960, 15 percent of drivers commuted out of their home county; in 2000, 25 percent did. Trip lengths are still relatively short on average, although that figure also has increased. In the early 1980s the average commute to work was about 8.5 miles, while today it is around 12 miles (data from 2001 National Highway Traffic Study, *ibid,* p. 51).

Building more lanes or advocating carpooling more are not going to solve our congestion problems; that is obvious to anyone dealing with road construction or counting the number of single-occupant cars on our city streets and regional highways. The costs of new road construction have skyrocketed along with the purchase price of the needed additional right-of-way. Protection of the environment and the socioeconomic fabric of our communities also have increased costs. While the number of cars on the road and length of our commutes have increased over the last 40 years, so has the need to repair and replace our existing, aging highways and bridges. Drivers silently endure rising gasoline prices, and they pay-out without much reduction in vehicle use. However, should the state or federal government propose raising fuel taxes to pay for road construction, people strongly object.

We can look forward to hydrogen-fueled cars, perhaps someday. However, it will take decades to develop the technology and build the generation and distribution system. People are moving back into the cities, closer to where they work. And mass transit systems are being built in many cities and across regions. All of it will take time and lots of public money.

---

*What if we all, or many of us, were to make a **little change**?*

So what is the answer? **<u>Think shrink!</u>** What if our cars were half the size they are today? We could put two cars side by side in one travel lane! What if we put the passenger behind the driver in tandem instead of beside the driver? We could then accommodate twice as many cars and move perhaps up to four times the number people in the space now taken up by one full-sized car with one driver.

The Tango seats two people in tandem.

Small <u>is</u> beautiful. And safe, if built right.

When traffic comes to a standstill in rush-hour traffic, how great would it be to travel down the lane stripe between stalled vehicles in one of these ultra-narrow vehicles? Changes in our traffic laws would be needed in some states to allow these movements, called lane splitting. And once you get to your destination and have to park, you can park four vehicles head to the curb in one parallel parking space.

Short cars, parked head or tail to the curb, use parking more efficiently.

Would you be surprised to learn that such cars now exist and are waiting for investors and buyers to fund mass production of them? Some are suitable for highway use, such as the Tango, and some, such as the BugE and GEM, are suitable only for city and neighborhood use. The GEM follows the modified golf cart model of electric vehicles. The BugE is a three-wheeled neighborhood electric vehicle (NEV) for one person with cargo space in the nose for grocery bags.

The BugE, a neighborhood electric vehicle by Blue Sky Design.

Cars such as the Smart and Think are less than standard width and length, and increase parking efficiency because of their size. However, because they still have side-by-side seating instead of tandem, there is less potential for improved space efficiency and congestion relief on existing roadways.

Recognition of such benefits is not new, only not acted upon by automakers. Management consulting firm Booz-Allen & Hamilton conducted a study in August 1993, "The Benefit and Cost Impacts of Implementing Commuter Cars in California" for the Institute of Transportation Studies, University of California at Berkeley. Their concept of the commuter car was an innovative three-wheeled vehicle that is comparable to a motorcycle in size but offers the advantages similar to an automobile in comfort, utility, and safety. It would be less than 4 feet wide, shorter than 12 feet, and approximately 4 feet high. The study concluded that as a result of implementing commuter cars, congestion in urban California cities would decrease, particularly if dedicated commuter car lanes were built. "Vehicle throughput is estimated to increase from 1 to 34 percent in the Bay Area for the low and high market penetration scenarios, respectively."

Another Booz-Allen & Hamilton report was "Study of Road Infrastructure Requirements for Innovative Vehicles" (August 1992). Mark Pitstick and William Garrison, of the UC Berkeley Institute of

Transportation Studies, reported on "Restructuring the Automobile/Highway System for Lean Vehicles: The Scaled Precedence Activity Network (SPAN) Approach" (April 1991). A related study was "Lean Vehicles: Strategies for Introduction Emphasizing Adjustments to Parking and Road Facilities" (SAE Technical Paper 901485). Among the studies' many favorable conclusions was that, "There are no insurmountable barriers in the infrastructure analysis that would preclude the introduction and success of the commuter car."

The Smart (left) and the Tango (right).

Ultra-narrow vehicles, such as the Tango and CLEVER (Compact Low Emission Vehicle for

Urban Transport), offer a better overall design, and are about the width of a motorcycle (42 inches or less) with all the creature comforts.

Advanced technology is the story of developing and applying the right tool for the right purpose to be used by someone in the right frame of mind.

It is the ultra-narrow vehicle (UNV), tandem-seated, electric-powered design that offers the best solution to problems of traffic congestion, road construction and maintenance costs, parking availability, fuel efficiency, and global warming. UNVs can increase the vehicle capacity per lane by 126 percent; for example, from 2000 vehicles per hour to 4,520 vehicles per hour. In a parking lot, restriping to accommodate UNVs would yield up to a 3.5:1 density increase.

Where will these cars come from? Who will make and sell them? Who will service them? For now, most of these UNVs and microvehicles must be built from available kits to be street legal. Mass production requires expensive tooling and crash testing first. You have to break them to make them.

Government subsidies would help, as the European Union has done developing the CLEVER. Nevertheless, the opportunities for new business ventures are immense as we add new alternatives based on new technologies and designs to our transportation system, such as the Segway personal transporter.

This is not to say that the large, conventionally sized sedans, trucks, and SUVs have to disappear.

The point is: pick the right vehicle for your trip. Own a big car, and own a small car (UNV). If you don't have 3, 4, or 5 passengers, or don't need to haul a lot of cargo, take your UNV! Perhaps a motorcycle, scooter, or a bicycle would do. Or walk or take mass transit. No more hogging the road!

Creature comforts of a car, the thrill of a motorcycle.

Visit:

www.commutercars.com

www.Fev-now.com

www.blueskydsn.com

www.clever-project.net

8. Motown Spirit

What Road to the Future?

America's automobile makers headquartered in Detroit were successful early the last century because of their innovation, automation, and assembly line methods. These manufacturers were adept at building cars to maximize their profits while meeting consumer demand. Much can happen in 20 years. In 1890, Henry Ford began to experiment with a "horseless carriage" and made his first powered-vehicle, which he called the

Quadricycle, in 1896. He started the Ford Motor Company in 1903. After introducing the popular Model T Ford in 1908, it took only 20 years for the Model T to make up 68 percent of all automobiles.

When gasoline was cheap, fuel efficiency and vehicle size were unimportant to most consumers. The long-term trend of increasing petroleum costs and global warming will shape consumer choices. In fact, they are rapidly changing already. Europe has dealt with high gasoline prices, including high fuel taxes, for many years; fuel efficiency and government standards are higher overseas. Because of high fuel costs, narrow streets, and heavy city congestion, small cars, such as the Smart car, have sold very well in Europe. Soon these cars will be imported to the United States and find increasing market share. Small cares such as the Honda Fit are already increasingly popular in the United States; however, the Fit is still too big and *doesn't have a tailored fit* for just one or two people. Even the Smart car, with its side-by-side seating instead of in tandem, *isn't smart enough.*

Recently, a company in India, Tata Motors, introduced the Nano, which it hopes to sell primarily as a second vehicle to the nation's 45 million motorcycle riders. Priced at just US$2,500, the Nano has a rear two-cylinder engine (33 hp) gets 46 miles per gallon, and can seat four to five people. Although it meets all safety requirements in India, cars for export to the US and Europe will need modifications. While economical and small, the design of the Nano is still not small enough.

Introduction of the Nano is but another example of interest in small, affordable cars, global markets, and shifting production to countries with very low labor costs. Renault produces an affordable car (the Logan) in countries including Colombia, Romania, Russia, India, and Iran. The VW group recently gave the go ahead to its design and engineering teams to develop a range of small cars. GM, Toyota and Ford are also developing low-cost cars.

Developing countries are having increasing traffic congestion problems, and as in the US, learning that it is difficult to build your way out of it. For example, the journey from south Mumbai, India, to the domestic airport took an hour and a half 10 years ago with a six-lane road. Despite widening it much more, it still takes the same time to commute the distance. A CAR study suggests 48 per cent of world demand for cars in 2020 will come from emerging countries. Last year the level was just 35.8 per cent. Worldwide car sales in 2007 were 57.6 million units. In a good year, the US market was worth 17 million cars and light trucks. Financing was plentiful and buyers wanted a new car every 2 years or so. If greenhouse gas emissions are to be reduced to desired levels worldwide, sales of new car with low carbon impact must increase dramatically.

Where does the future of the automobile lie? Detroit has tried but has been slow to innovate and get ahead of the trend. Ford abandoned production of the electric Think at its Norway facilities; new investors have purchased rights to the car and are gearing up production of an improved model. GM also gave up on production of its electric vehicle, the EV-1. The six major automakers of the world

(GM, Ford, Daimler-Chrysler, Toyota, Honda, and Nissan) engaged in electric car experimental models in the 1990's in response to the California Air Resources Board (CARB) zero-emission vehicle (ZEV) mandate, which would have required 10 percent of sales be ZEVs. Several companies later challenged requirements in court and reduced their impacts. Less than 1,000 electric vehicles were built to comply with the initial requirements; then the manufacturers claimed there was no consumer demand, in spite of waiting lists for them. Granted, the cars did have problems with battery life. Cheap lead-acid batteries, although ideal for short distance commuting, were found to have inadequate range for family use in large cars. During that time, Toyota and Honda also were busy developing hybrid power plants, which have sold surprisingly well in the American market. GM and Ford entered the market late but are now building hybrids for several models.

GM recently announced plans for production of another electric vehicle, the Chevy Volt. This is a full-sized car with what GM calls an innovative on-board battery recharging system using a small internal combustion engine (ICE). Fuel efficiency would be high; the design is "sexy" and responds to consumer demand. But space wise, it's still a road hog and feeds the "muscle car" mentality.

New automakers are springing up to build electric sports cars and trucks with much-improved range over earlier models, taking advantage of recent advances in lithium-ion batteries and nanotechnology. Altairnano has developed a novel nano-structured lithium titanate anode material, to enable environmentally safe batteries of longer life and quicker recharge.

Electric cars are coming again!

Tesla Motors, Wrightspeed, Phoenix Motors, and the Lightning Car Company are moving toward limited production of very expensive electric vehicles, which in time may evolve into more affordable models. But look at their size. *Nothing new.*

The Detroit Auto Show and others around the country never live up to claims of revolutionary advances. For years the major automobile makers have shown a different cut of suit on basically the same big, muscle-bound body. How about a slimmed down version for modern times?

Charging for parking by the square foot would incentivize small cars.

Besides auto shows, the industry is participating in contests, such as the Automotive X PRIZE, for innovative vehicles, sponsored by the X PRIZE Foundation and other organizations and businesses. The goal of this contest, due to start in 2008, is to inspire a new generation of viable, super-efficient vehicles that will help break our addiction to oil and reduce the effects of climate change. The multimillion dollar purse will be awarded likely by 2010 to the teams that win a stage race for clean, production-capable vehicles that exceed 100 miles per gallon equivalent fuel economy. The competition is being planned for travel through multiple cities in 2009-2010 while broadcasting to a global audience, building consumer demand for vehicles in the competition and demonstrating many practical, clean, and affordable vehicle options.

X PRIZE jurors include leaders of the nation's top environmental organizations, including Carl Pope, executive director of the Sierra Club; Christopher Flavin, president of Worldwatch Institute; Jean-Michel Cousteau, president of Ocean Futures Society; and Jonathan Lash, President of the World Resources Institute. Also, Jay Leno noted auto enthusiast and host of the "Tonight Show" as well as automotive icon Carroll Shelby join four Green Car Journal editors to round out the 2008 jury.

Will Motown embrace the spirit of its early days and leap frog ahead, or will it stay stuck focused on building road hogs? Some decisions in the not-too-distant past are not encouraging. Besides earlier abandonment of electric car production, GM has shown reluctance to help bring ultra-narrow vehicles into production. In 2002, GM declined "to enter into any financially supportive role" with Commuter Cars Corporation. "It is not in GM's best interest to pursue this," said L.D. Burns, V.P. Research & Development and Planning (March 14, 2002 letter to Rick Woodbury). Detroit has a history of missed opportunities, decline in market share, government subsidy for recovery, and relative profitability, in a 10-year cycle it seems. The latest recovery has been built on the boom of SUVs and minivans, and a base of American's love of pick-up trucks. Former Chrysler chairman Lee Iacocca, with some vision, has led production of the GEM car. Now hybrid cars have caught America's fancy, first offered by Toyota and Honda. Will the Smart car be next? Is there hope that GM or Ford would leap ahead with production of an ultra-narrow, electric powered car? Probably not without a push or pull from the federal or California government, if past history is any indication. Perhaps VW or Renault, with the monetary strength of the Euro behind them, or China, will be the first to enter with gusto the UNV market in the United States and world.

Visit:

www.lightningcarcompany.com

www.altairnano.com

http://auto.xprize.org

www.teslamotors.com

www.commutercars.com

9. Uncle Sam's Garage

At a Convenient Location Near You

U.S. Transportation Secretary Norman Mineta has written:

> "Congestion is not a fact of life. We need a new approach and we need it now. Congestion results from poor policy choices and failure to separate solutions that are effective and those that are not. ...We must not be afraid to embrace new solutions if we

are going to make any meaningful progress on reducing congestion. ...The bottom line is that every person and every business in America has a vested in interest in reducing congestion. ...We have the tools, the technology, and the plan to make today's congestion a thing of the past." (*National Strategy to Reduce Congestion on America's Transportation*)

In spite of much talk, progress toward reducing congestion remains elusive.

The TRB Committee on Freeway Operations ("Freeway Operations in 2000 and Beyond," *Transportation in the New Millenium*, 2000) has stated:

"A comprehensive freeway corridor traffic management (FCTM) program requires a combination of approaches, techniques, systems, and operating policies aimed at establishing and maintaining a balance between highway capacity and vehicular demand.

"Travel on the freeway infrastructure is a valuable commodity, and the change in philosophy that leads to this understanding will take some time. Roadway pricing and toll roadways are the first steps in this transition."

Both the public and private sectors of our economy need a paradigm shift in thinking and investment, which can lead to a new system of passenger and freight transportation in America that would be a model for the world. A change is needed that is comparable to development of the information superhighway and miniaturization of electronic devices during the last 20 years.

The imperative is to reduce greenhouse gas emissions, traffic congestion, and infrastructure costs while enhancing efficiency, safety, and mobility. New models of transportation would be good for our economy, although requiring some transition and adjustments in the overall products and services of the automobile industry. Electric motors simply do not require as many parts or as much service as internal combustion engines.

Changes in the vehicle types, management of our highways, and adoption of intelligent transportation system technologies would be consistent with proposals from such transportation industry representatives as the Association of Road and Transportation Builders Association (ARTBA). The ARTBA Board of Directors on September 28, 2006 endorsed a task force proposal regarding "Critical Commerce Corridors" to upgrade and build a new generation of transportation infrastructure that would separate commercial freight traffic from passenger vehicles. ARTBA Chairman Michael Walton has testified (November 16, 2006) before the National Surface Transportation & Policy Revenue Study Commission on Meeting the Nation's Surface Transportation Needs that:

> "Only the federal government can coordinate all parts of the U.S. surface transportation system to implement a

holistic approach to the nation's transportation challenges."

Indeed, such changes also would be consistent with such federal legislation as the Transportation Efficiency Act for the 21st Century (TEA-21) and its subsequent versions of re-enactment, the Safe, Accountable, Flexible, Efficient Transportation Equity Act: A Legacy for Users 2005 (SAFETEA-LU).

Efficiency is the key word. To change our old ways is the challenge.

The federal government of the United States can play a key role by relaxing import and manufacturing restrictions on innovative vehicles, subsidizing crash tests, increasing fuel-efficiency (CAFÉ) standards, supporting mass transit systems, encouraging production of alternative-fueled vehicles (renewable energy sources), and investing in domestic renewable energy facilities rather than securing foreign oil resources through military might. Speed limits that increase fuel efficiency and thus reduce greenhouse gas emissions can be mandated.

Corporate Average Fuel Economy (CAFE) is the sales weighted average fuel economy, expressed in miles per gallon (mpg), of a manufacturer's fleet of passenger cars or light trucks with a gross vehicle weight rating (GVWR) of 8,500 lbs. or less, manufactured for sale in the United States, for any given model year. It was in response to the 1973-74 Arab oil embargo that the "Energy Policy Conservation Act," enacted into law by Congress in 1975, added Title V, "Improving Automotive Efficiency," to the Motor Vehicle Information and Cost Savings Act and established CAFE standards for passenger cars and light trucks. The near-term goal was to double new car fuel economy by model year 1985. Recent CAFÉ standards passed by Congress still are not adequate to address the global warming crisis. Standards should be increased at least another 15 mpg during the next 15 years, in addition to other federal actions.

A report by the Urban Land Institute (Ewing et al., 2007), "Growing Cooler: The Evidence on Urban Development and Climate Change," calls for three federal actions:

- Federal climate change legislation should require regional transportation plans to pass a conformity test for carbon dioxide emissions, similar to those for other criteria pollutants.

- Enact "Green-TEA" transportation legislation that reduces GHGs, bringing a paradigm shift that could further address environmental performance, climate protection, and green development through greater emphasis on alternatives to our present transportation system and community planning.

- Provide funding directly to metropolitan planning organizations (MPOs), which contain 80 percent of the nation's population and 85 percent of its economic output. Current investment by state transportation departments in metropolitan areas lags far behind these percentages. MPOs should be given authority to decide how funds would be spent.

Across the board, in all components of our transportation system, we need incentives and disincentives to encourage decisions by manufacturers and consumers that will support the attainment of much greater efficiency in moving people and products. Without significant progress to such change in the next 10 years, we will have set the planet on an irreversible course of warming for another 100 years.

Active traffic management strategies, allowing designated and restricted uses of travel lanes, need to be approved, funded, and implemented by the federal government. Construction of additional lanes will only increase vehicle miles traveled and increase GHG emissions until our fleet of vehicles is replaced with non-carbon based fuels. In 15 years, all new vehicles sold should have zero carbon emissions.

State and local governments can enact legislation allowing a wider variety of vehicles to use the roadways, and travel between lanes (lane-splitting) and two-abreast in lanes. Legislation has been introduced in some states, such as in Washington and Oregon in 2003, to define ultra-narrow vehicles and allow lane splitting but was never enacted.

States could revise their vehicle registration categories to provide an incentive for people to purchase at least one small vehicle for commuting purposes. Registration fees could be higher for extra large vehicles and those with big gas-guzzling engines. Four-cylinders are really enough to get you anywhere; fees could be higher for non-commercial registrations of vehicles with 6, 8, and 10 cylinder engines.

At the federal level, past proposals have been made regarding provisions of reauthorizing the federal highway bill, which still need to be passed today. For TEA-21 in 2003, Rick Woodbury, President of Commuter Cars Corporation, proposed several incentives the federal government could create for little cost that would encourage commuters to make responsible choices when choosing their mode of transportation to work or the store:

- Define ultra-narrow vehicles (UNVs) as any vehicle having a maximum width of 42-inches from mirror to mirror.

- Paint a stripe down the center of a lane, such as an HOV lane, to designate it as two lanes to be used by UNVs and motorcycles.

- Allow straddling the painted line between lanes (lane splitting) by UNVs and motorcycles during heavy congestion and slowed traffic. (As has been legal in California for more than 30 years.)

- Allow UNVs access to HOV lanes regardless of vehicle occupancy.

- Fund studies for developing ideas to maximize the rate of transition to UNVs and to identify highway corridors where congestion could best be relieved by UNVs.

- Fund studies to explore the potential of trains carrying UNVs on flatbead cars for long distances.

Academia and the Transportation Research Board also could study the impacts on congestion of commuters driving UNVs. The Automotive X

PRIZE for innovative vehicles will receive support from the U.S. Department of Energy and Argonne National Laboratory; the U.S. Department of Transportation's National Highway, Traffic and Safety Administration (NHTSA) and Federal Highway Administration (FHA); the U.S. Environmental Protection Agency's Office of Transportation and Air Quality (OTAQ); and the California Air Resources Board (CARB). The federal government, in addition, could subsidize production of new vehicle types and place large orders to replace existing federal vehicle fleets.

Unfortunately, the vision of the federal government, which aligns with Detroit, is that the future automobile will be as large as present and require a comparably large power source. The federal government is looking long-term at hydrogen powered fuel-cell technology as the answer. However, the time scale for implementation of such a transformation does not address the rate of global warming.

The Vehicle Technologies Program of the U.S. Department of Energy leads the FreedomCAR and Fuel Partnership program. The Partnership is a collaborative effort among DOE, energy companies BP America, Chevron Corporation, ConocoPhillips, Exxon Mobil Corporation, and Shell Hydrogen (US), and the U.S. Council for Automotive Research (USCAR) partners (DaimlerChrysler Corporation, Ford Motor Company, and General Motors Corporation).

The partners jointly conduct technology roadmapping, determine technical requirements, suggest research and development (R&D) priorities, and monitor the R&D activities necessary to achieve the goals of the Partnership. The partnership examines the pre-competitive, high-risk research needed to develop the component and infrastructure technologies necessary to enable a full range of affordable cars and light trucks, and the fueling infrastructure for them that will reduce the dependence of the nation's personal transportation system on imported oil and minimize harmful vehicle emissions, without sacrificing freedom of mobility and freedom of vehicle choice.

The "Freedom" principle is framed by:

- Freedom from dependence on imported oil;

- Freedom from pollutant emissions;

- Freedom for Americans to choose the kind of vehicle they want to drive, and to drive where they want, when they want; and

- Freedom to obtain fuel affordably and conveniently.

The partners have established challenging high-level technical goals and timetables for research and development (R&D) to accelerate advancements in technologies that enable reduced oil consumption and increased energy efficiency in passenger vehicles.

The Partnership addresses:

- Integrated systems analysis

- Fuel cell power systems

- Hydrogen storage systems

- Technologies for the production and distribution of hydrogen necessary for the viability of hydrogen vehicles

- The technical basis for codes and standards to support hydrogen vehicles and infrastructure and the interface between them

- Electric propulsion systems applicable to both fuel cell and internal combustion/electric hybrid vehicles (e.g., power electronics, electric motors)

- Lightweight materials

- Electrical energy storage systems (e.g., batteries, power capacitors)

- Advanced combustion and emission control systems for internal combustion engines (employing a variety of fuels such as diesel, hydrogen, and renewable blends, and investigating innovative concepts such as homogeneous charge compression ignition systems, variable compression ratio, in-cylinder exhaust gas recirculation, etc.)

The time to act is now.

In conclusion, it is time we quit driving an oversized, mostly empty hay wagon to town when riding a horse would do. We need greater efficiency in our transportation system, which can come from different power systems and sizes of vehicles. There is too much waste in the weight and size or our cars.

That is not to say that all cars need be small. Most people own two cars today. Keep the large one for family trips and carpooling. The other one needs to be a narrow, one- or two-seater that takes less space on our highways and emits much less carbon dioxide and other pollutants than the typical big car.

In a paper titled, "Using Technology and Partnerships to Create More Efficient, Equitable, and Environmentally Sound Transportation," (TRB Paper 00078, *Transportation in the New Millenium*, 2000) authors Salon, Sperling, Shaheen, and Sturges of the UC Davis Institute of Transportation Studies argue that the successful introduction of new mobility alternatives requires a systematic integration between technology and policy, resulting in synergistic benefits of cost and convenience to the user. They acknowledge that for new options to be economically attractive, households generally must choose to reduce the number of conventional vehicles by one or more.

Contact Uncle Sam today.

Tell your Congressional representatives that you want programs fully funded and laws enacted that support efficiency in our transportation system. Talk to your state and local political leaders, too. Remove the roadblocks to innovation.

In the meantime, leave your car at home and take mass transit, when it is available and appropriate. Or ride a bicycle or walk. Or join a carpool. Once a week, try something different for getting to/from work besides driving your car.

Resolve to cut your own carbon dioxide load by at least 20 percent. Do your part.

Quit hogging the road.

About the Author

Olin T. Gideonson is an environmental planner and technical writer who has worked in the consulting engineering services industry for more than 20 years. His current interests include renewable energy, land use, and transportation planning as they relate to climate change. He is a long-time resident of the Cascadia Bioregion in the Pacific Northwest.